The Simple Guide to Child Trauma

The Simple Guide to Child Trauma

What It Is and How to Help

BETSY DE THIERRY

Illustrated by Emma Reeves

Jessica Kingsley *Publishers*
London and Philadelphia

First published in 2017
by Jessica Kingsley Publishers
73 Collier Street
London N1 9BE, UK
and
400 Market Street, Suite 400
Philadelphia, PA 19106, USA

www.jkp.com

Library of Congress Cataloging in Publication Data
Names: Thierry, Betsy de, author.
Title: The simple guide to child trauma : what it is and how to help / Betsy
    de Thierry ; illustrated by Emma Reeves.
Description: London ; Philadelphia : Jessica Kingsley Publishers, 2017. |
    Includes bibliographical references and index.
Identifiers: LCCN 2016018703 | ISBN 9781785921360 (alk. paper)
Subjects: LCSH: Psychic trauma in children. | Psychic trauma in
    children--Treatment.
Classification: LCC RJ506.P66 T45 2017 | DDC 618.92/8521--dc23 LC
record available at
https://urldefense.proofpoint.com/v2/url?u=https-
3A__lccn.loc.gov_2016018703&d=BQIFAg&c=euGZstcaTDllvimEN8b7jXr
wqOf-v5A_CdpgnVfiiMM&r=1v35CMXDPq9tusP6l-19m3h61RNMvLridz
O13DRUbWg&m=jjYOjGFiMRD-pIG38b1JRSav9yL12jDGF2d2bOJUPJs
&s=U3rPFAHYYEBAcieEhO0qVExsWiTqjWLHyDr1PpYAgE4&e=

British Library Cataloguing in Publication Data
A CIP catalogue record for this book is available from the British Library

ISBN 978 1 78592 136 0
eISBN 978 1 78450 401 4

Printed and bound in the United States

This book is dedicated to the lost souls whom no one understood until now.

May they know hope for their future and a life filled with love.

CONTENTS

FOREWORD

I was invited by Betsy de Thierry to speak about attachment research to colleagues at her Trauma Recovery Centre in Bath. I arrived early and she kindly gave me a guided tour. Naturally, I only saw empty rooms but I was enchanted by the different spaces that I entered, where traumatised children (and sometimes adults) can express themselves in myriad ways, to find resolution, repair and peace from their torments. There were quiet rooms, private rooms, rooms where a child could really let rip; there were opportunities for them to write things – anything they wanted – on the walls, and there were some big structures where they could lose (and find) themselves, along with a seemingly endless supply of dolls, clay, mobiles, toys…you name it, there it was.

This is a Tardis of a book, where you will find the distilled thoughts and tips of a life spent with children traumatised by abuse, horrific events, accidents and seemingly unbearable loss. Betsy gives us an authentic feel for what it's like for a child when suddenly they can't think straight, and not know why; she helps us to appreciate how such a child can be on red alert all the time; and you will gain a powerful understanding of how a traumatised child can kick off and lose control without much warning.

This is not a standard 'toolkit'; there is a burgeoning repository of 'direct work' toolkits available elsewhere, which reflects a growing interest from practitioners desperate to connect with the 'inner worlds' of children. The problem with some toolkits is that, without theoretical anchor points and research bearings, they can seem marooned. But in this simple guide you will find lots of useful ideas, which Betsy locates within an evidence-based and theoretically informed framework.

What this guide does elegantly and quickly is bring a large amount of research – from psychology, social work, neuroscience, biochemistry and genetics – directly to the busy but interested parents and carers and professionals working in this field. It translates complex ideas into 'practice-rich' language for adults who need to understand the inner worlds of children, rather than simply explore their wishes and feelings. It's also quick and easy to read – I've now read it three times, and I've gained new and different insights each time... Enjoy!

Professor David Shemmings OBE

INTRODUCTION

This book is written to help those adults who really want to see the children in their care recover from the tough life experiences that they have had. It can be exhausting looking after traumatised children because they are so full of hurt and pain but it is also life changing when there are clear signs of recovery and healing.

This is a little guide to help those who care about children and young people explore how people respond to trauma because it seems to be quite a foundational thing to grasp and yet it is not a common thing to be taught or spoken about. It shouldn't add more guilt to the demands, expectations and workload that many of us carry but should instead shed some light on behaviour, feelings and reactions that can create confusion and further pain, which then leads to less stress!

We'll have a look at what trauma is, how children and young people respond to such experiences and how they then affect us.

The book concludes with some ideas and practical suggestions of how to help the children recover from trauma rather than letting it affect them all of their life. It isn't a manual but just a simple overview!

So it's a book designed to bring hope! It brings some practical suggestions, which could be applied to your setting, whether that's a home where you have all been traumatised, if you are caring for traumatised children in a professional setting or if you are fostering or looking after traumatised children.

The information here should subsequently mean less stress and turmoil for everyone!

Chapter 1

UNDERSTANDING TRAUMA

To begin with we are going to explore what trauma is and how it affects all of us in our emotions, behaviour, learning and relationships.

This can help us to help children and young people recover from the challenging experiences that life has thrown at them and maybe also help you as an adult to know how to recover yourself if you need to.

Stress, crisis and trauma

There is a difference between stress, crisis and trauma.

Most children have *stress* and this can become a positive experience that fuels momentum and learning if it's limited to short, sharp bursts for specific reasons like a new experience or a performance.

Crisis is something that many children experience, but with emotional support and a primary caregiver helping to navigate the child through it, there doesn't have to be any negative consequences that last long term.

What is trauma?

A really helpful definition of trauma has been written by experts at the Institute of Recovery from Childhood Trauma: 'Trauma is an event or series of events such as abuse, maltreatment, neglect or tragedy that causes a profound experience of helplessness leading to terror' (IRCT, 2015).

Trauma shatters our sense of safety, stability, trust and innocence.

Trauma is toxic stress. Toxic stress is created when the trauma is prolonged and where the child is powerless and can't change the continually frightening experience. It can impact a child immediately in the short term and can cause impact in the long term unless there is an appropriate response given to help the child recover.

Let's look at how trauma impacts us all. We'll also be looking later on at the kind of responses that facilitate recovery – because we can all help people recover!

Children soak up what's around them

It's pretty tough for the adults who care, but sadly children and young people soak up what's going on around them – even if it's non-verbal, such as an atmosphere of intense anxiety or fear in the home.

This can be really hard to read and think about as it can often make us adults feel bad about 'not being perfect'. However, it's important to understand how children and young people become traumatised so that we can work with them to see them recover and have a future that is not impacted by things that they have seen, heard and experienced.

The fact that you are reading this means that you are a caring person who really wants the children in your care to do well in life.

Maybe you want the children in your world to have opportunities that you didn't have yourself and you want them to know love and value even if you didn't experience that when you were young.

What kind of things can cause trauma to affect children?

Children become traumatised in any environment where fear is a theme. They soak in the atmosphere where the adults are angry, aggressive, uncaring or emotionally distant.

They pick up on 'emotionally frozen' atmospheres where the adults don't feel comfortable with feelings being expressed, and they end up developing ways to cope with a need to connect emotionally.

They pick up on tense, anxious atmospheres and either become anxious themselves or develop ways of coping with the anxious atmosphere using coping mechanisms, which could be all sorts of things such as risk-taking behaviours or being emotionally shut down.

Children pick up on angry, aggressive atmospheres, even when they don't see any violence or anger. They feel it and internalise it and it can then 'leak' out of them in their behaviour in some way.

They can be traumatised because they have experienced a bad, scary, nasty or upsetting event once and have no adult to help support them through it. Sometimes they can get stuck in that moment of time internally and still feel scared and shocked years later.

When a child experiences a lack of care and emotional connection that enable them to blossom and grow, then they can feel deep sadness, loneliness and fear. Those strong feelings can only go if someone helps them.

A child is traumatised when things happen around them that cause them terror and they don't have an adult to help them, guide them and process with them what happened and how they felt.

A child can become traumatised if they are abused by an adult who is meant to be caring for them and then they feel too afraid to tell anyone. They don't speak about what happened and may even say that they feel fine if they are asked. They may even smile and laugh (often traumatised children do this as a mask to hide their real fears) but inside could be living in terror of someone finding out and hurting them even more. The abuse usually leaves them with feelings of shame and embarrassment and they often think it is their own fault, but it's never the fault of a child.

A child can become traumatised when they seek out an adult to share their book, toy, news, worries or thoughts with and they are repetitively rejected, told to 'go away', shouted at, pushed away or told that they are irritating and they need to be quiet and less annoying.

The child interprets that they must be bad and must either try harder to be accepted and loved or they may express their hurt through behaviour that seems to have 'no reason'. Sometimes the child assumes they are so bad, because they are not listened to, that they try and hurt themselves and feel physical pain to numb the intense feelings of sadness, loneliness and rejection.

A child can become traumatised when they have a parent who struggles with mental illness and is sometimes nurturing and yet sometimes very needy, aggressive, angry or depressed and unable to nurture them. When the child feels frightened of the parent's anger or aggression and also has to take on the role of carer for the mentally ill parent, then the child can end up confused and deeply scared.

A child can become traumatised when they are left crying in their cot as babies for hours, needing someone to cuddle them and help them. That helplessness and isolation can impact a little one and leave them confused and untrusting of adults because they were so powerless and dependent on others and were let down. They may become controlling or angry or hoard food to try and be independent.

They may struggle in friendships, as they have learnt from a pre-language age that they shouldn't trust anyone, although they probably wouldn't be able to communicate that feeling in words.

A child becomes traumatised when they lie in bed at night repeatedly hearing the sounds of shouting, bangs, crashes and screams and they have no idea what is happening but they are filled with terror.

A child can become traumatised when they are misunderstood as naughty and defiant when actually they feel confused by their own behaviour too but don't know how to contain their anger and hurt. They can just end up feeling increasing shame about their behaviour that they can't seem to control.

A child can become traumatised when they are called names and told that they are 'mistakes', 'stupid' or 'worthless'. Those words make a psychological scar and cause them to believe that they are bad people.

Sometimes they then live 'up to' those words and prove that they are bad and sometimes they can spend their whole life trying to prove that they are not bad…

Children can be traumatised when bad things happen that couldn't be avoided – homes that are lost, families that are split apart due to conflict or disaster or lack of food or clothes or people who care for them.

Sometimes children feel invisible, as if no one cares about them. Sadly, sometimes this can be true. This leads to an emptiness and sadness that can echo deep in their insides, and they end up resigned to a life of disappointment and lack of love.

When children have been this hurt and let down, it can be hard to receive love, as it seems so unnatural to them. These little lives need consistent care and love even if they seem to reject the adults and appear to not care. That hard exterior that they present is just their self-defensiveness that they needed to use in order to survive and it's hard for them to just 'drop the armour'. If your child behaves in this way, try not to take it personally and keep on trying to support them and connect with them.

Children find words really tough to use

Traumatic experiences have an impact on children. It's not true that 'kids just get over it' as they are resilient. Sadly, experiencing trauma changes the brain of a child and this can lead to changes in thoughts, behaviour, relationships, ability to learn or focus and emotional responses.

Children will be unlikely to be able to use words to describe these changes. Words can be difficult to use when someone is traumatised because the part of the brain that is responsible for speech and language goes 'offline' when there are high levels of stress.

In fact, that's why we often reply 'I'm fine thanks' when people ask us how we are – because it can be hard to find words or even reflect on how we are!

Instead of using words, children will usually respond subconsciously to the experience(s) and this often shows in their behaviour and emotions.

This means that we need to be especially careful with traumatised children because they will usually be scared by what's just happened to them, will often struggle to trust adults and will feel overwhelmed and confused about their feelings and behaviour and the consequences of that.

They often don't know or understand themselves that their behaviour and changes in relationships, thoughts and feelings are because of what has happened to them. It's our job as adults to help them to understand so they feel less awkward, ashamed or shocked.

The good news is that with the right care and support, the child's brain can heal and they can recover from the experiences that they have endured. *They can recover.*

What can you do when children have become traumatised?

Children need emotional connection with adults and children where they feel safe, cared for and known. They need adults to regularly spend time speaking to them in ways that are not intense but are playful and also meaningful.

Children who have been traumatised can struggle with different things and often need the help of adults in more ways than those who were not traumatised.

Traumatised children can often end up behaving in ways that are actually familiar to them, where their subconscious is replicating the early, often horrific and frightening, relational experiences they had. For example, Matilda (age nine) used to feel scared when someone told her what to do in a strong voice and so she immediately shouted, using aggressive, threatening words and actions as an instinctive response to the feelings of powerlessness. This could be due to her not understanding her strong feelings of fear and acting in a way that felt familiar to her when someone was upset.

This can be really tough when an adult wants to care for them, as they can sometimes seem rejecting, controlling, dominating or uninterested towards the adult. Traumatised children's strong, subconscious emotions that are not thought through can be overwhelming for those caring for them. But as they settle into an environment of nurture, consistency, predictability and kindness where they can explore their powerful emotions, they can recover and become strong.

Sadly, some schools and the adults working with children in all sorts of different settings can reward children for *not* showing their emotions but instead 'bottling them up'.

One of my sons was given a sticker for not crying when he fell over at school. I chatted to him and he explained that he 'swallowed it down and was brave'. I explained that it was important to cry and express the strong feelings at school too or he would get an emotional tummy ache after a while, even an emotional constipation!

What we know about the process of swallowing down emotions and not expressing them is that it is really bad for our health. We need to validate and acknowledge the strong feelings and, in the context of a safe relationship, work out ways to express strong emotions where people don't get hurt.

There are chapters at the end of the book that suggest activities to do with the children in your care which will help to strengthen your relationship so that it can be a safe place to explore these strong feelings. Maybe you could make something with them, cook with them or play a game with them.

While you are doing that you could speak gently about the atmosphere in the home and how you'd like it to be. Maybe ask your child to draw a picture or write a few thoughts about how they'd love their home to be.

That could be quite an intimidating thing to do but it could help you to do something to start the process of seeing some positive change come to the family home.

Jane was traumatised as a child because she was born into a family where they were only just coping. Mum was juggling her two young sisters and her and also trying to work, when she could. She was dependent on the salary of her partner and on him being able to be around regularly so that she could attend work. Her partner, Jim, was a man who was emotionally distant and struggling with the demands of a growing family. He didn't like the children to make a noise and was angry towards them. Jim controlled the money in the home and so the children lived a life with only just enough food, just enough clothes and very stressed parents. Jane grew up frightened of her dad's anger and was always trying to help her mum cope. She would often care for her mum by doing chores and listening to her talk about her anxieties, and she was often trying to support her. This meant that Jane didn't experience a childhood free from worry and stress but felt immense responsibility from an early age. She learned not to trust adults and instead be self-reliant. This meant that she didn't find friendships easy and was often seen as a loner. She internalised all her feelings and became depressed and withdrawn. Her teachers began to be worried, as she was often glazed over and rarely seemed engaged in her lessons. After spending a year and a half seeing a therapist each week she was able to articulate how sad she had been feeling and they began to explore and process some of the frightening times that had caused Jane to get stuck inside. Soon she felt so much better, less fearful, more confident and able to voice her needs.

Chapter 2

THE IMPACT OF TRAUMA

Most people would agree that children find it helpful to understand what is happening to them when they respond to trauma but, of course, that is only possible when the adults who are caring for them understand it too.

The fact is that our bodies respond to trauma by essentially setting off alarms internally that make us able to have energy or run away or freeze as a response to the threat. This is meant to help us to survive, but when someone has been repeatedly scared or emotionally overwhelmed when they were little and dependent on adults to meet their needs and they don't get their survival brain soothed and calmed, they begin to form a brain that is almost always wired on hyper alert because the world seems to be so scary.

This 'threat response' is important to understand because it helps children know that when they have a physical and emotional response to trauma, they are not being naughty or strange but responding in a way that is expected. As adults, our response is the same!

It is good to remember that, when any of us feels threatened, we naturally respond with this 'fight, flight or freeze' response, usually without noticing it.

So let's unpack this response a bit so that we can see how it affects us and the children who have been traumatised. The 'fight, flight or freeze' response is sometimes called the 'threat response' and it is based in our brainstem, which is the area of the brain near the back of the neck. This is where our most basic responses like breathing and heart rate are based. In fact, it's the only area of the brain that is fully formed when a baby is born.

This area is linked to another area in the brain called the 'limbic system', which, if faced with something it feels is a threat, makes our emotions respond with panic. Doing so releases hormones to prepare and enable our bodies to run (flight), hide (freeze) or scream loudly or physically fight (fight).

Meanwhile, when this threat response happens, the ability to think, be rational, negotiate or reflect goes 'offline'. The rational part of the brain is the front part and is called the 'prefrontal cortex'. This was first called 'the triune brain' as it talks about the brain being in these three parts.

So when a person is faced with threat or what their subconscious thinks is threat, their brainstem responds with a survival threat response (fight, flight, freeze) and causes the emotional brain – the limbic system – to release hormones ready for action. A part of this emotional brain – the amygdala – sets the whole brain into a panic alarm response system. We tell the children that it's as if the brainstem catches fire due to threat and the limbic brain has a smoke alarm (the amygdala) that has been set off and makes a huge disruptive noise to make sure there is an appropriate response to the threat!

The other area of the brain that goes 'offline' when this threat response is activated is the 'Broca's' area, which is responsible for speech and language. That's why it can be really difficult to express how we feel in words when we've just experienced something really awful.

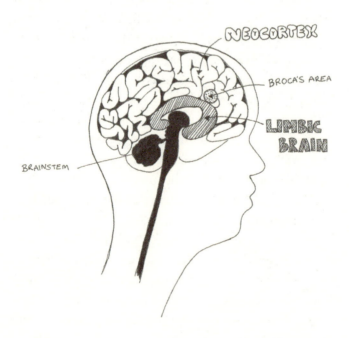

If the traumatic experience happens repeatedly then it would be normal for the child to live in a continual state of threat. This then makes it really difficult for the child to think, reason, negotiate or reflect, as that part of the brain is not working well due to the amount of hormones pumping around the child's body and the feelings of terror that are dominating the child's internal world. This is called the 'prolonged threat response' because the brain gets stuck in a response to possible threat all the time.

So, to sum up, the threat response impacts a child's behaviour, their feelings and their relationships because they don't feel safe but instead feel threatened, scared, confused and unstable.

The only way to enable a child to recover is to help them feel calm and safe by being a safe person who can support and help them.

When a person has been hurt in a relationship, they can only be healed in a relationship.

How does trauma affect behaviour, relationships, learning, thinking, feeling and doing?

Trauma impacts a child's relationships because when someone they know has hurt them, either on purpose or because they were nearby when an awful thing happened, the child is left with questions and confusion around trust.

When a child is around events or relationships that make them feel scared, and they are not sure who to trust and how to relate to adults or other children, this can lead to other problems like loneliness, isolation, bullying or – worse still – being exploited.

Trauma impacts the child's emotions, as they don't have enough internal 'space' to hold all the negative feelings that they feel.

They don't know what to do with these feelings and they end up 'leaking' their feelings by behaving in ways that even disappoint them at first. This negative behaviour, which is actually a way of communicating that they need help, often causes them to be labelled as 'defiant', 'bad' or 'naughty', and then they are often treated as if they are naughty or bad.

This can make them feel bad inside, rejected and worthless. They can eventually lose the ability to see their gifts or talents and just see themselves as others see them because of their behaviour.

Feelings of low self-esteem can lead to feelings of depression or anxiety. A child may end up trying so hard to prove that they are good that they become a perfectionist or they may just act up to the label and get naughtier and naughtier.

They could end up self-harming or engaging in dangerous activities to take risks because they feel so numb and sad inside. Drugs and alcohol can be tempting because they give highs that make them feel alive and can also numb the internal pain. The world can be too scary and rejecting, so a world full of drink and drugs can be more tolerable – even though, of course, this leads to further complications and problems.

Children can often hide their vulnerability by acting angry or tough or like they don't care. But they do care. It's just a way of protecting themselves because they are so used to be being rejected and mistreated, so they can rarely trust someone enough to show them how scared or sad they feel. Sometimes it feels like they have built a wall around themselves so that they can't feel the pain so much and no one can come too close to them. It can be hard to get out of a 'cycle of trauma' because, once it's happened, these emotions are so strong that unless adults help the child, they will behave in ways that lead to other behaviours that impact on relationships, learning, self-esteem, an understanding of the world and future decisions.

Children and young people are dependent on adults understanding this and offering skilled and effective support to enable them to break the trauma cycle and to process – think and talk through – their strong feelings.

It is recognised that 'trauma is perhaps the most avoided, ignored, belittled, denied, misunderstood, and untreated cause of human suffering' (Levine and Kline, 2007, p.3). This means that currently a lot of professionals working with traumatised children and young people aren't always trained to know what trauma symptoms are and how to help reduce them.

The more of us who learn about trauma and speak about it, the safer our communities will be for those who need to be understood and need to recover.

If a child is in hospital with a serious illness it is often straightforward for the child to ask for support and for the adult to be able to verbalise support and are, but when a child has been abused, neglected or suffered significant loss sometimes the people around them can feel afraid to say anything in case they 'get it wrong' and so the family can feel lonely and isolated.

There is now strong evidence that shows us that unprocessed trauma (trauma that isn't talked about and is bottled up or repressed) can lead to increased mental health difficulties during adulthood and a host of social problems, such as drug use, school difficulties, anti-social behaviour, etc.

It can also lead to other problems, such as post-traumatic stress disorder (PTSD), conduct disorders and dissociative disorders, and unprocessed trauma can even lead to medical challenges, such as asthma and heart disease (Perry and Szalavitz, 2011).

But, when trauma is processed in the context of a warm and genuine relationship, the impact is minimalised if not altogether transformed into greater resilience and so can totally change the degree of impact on the child and their future.

What fires together, wires together

Anyone who has experienced trauma can be 'triggered' by anything that is linked in their subconscious to their trauma experience. This can cause sudden behaviour or an emotional outburst, which can be a threat response, and is often seen as illogical.

It is impossible for our subconscious to work out when a threat is real or perceived. These seemingly illogical responses only stop once they have been thought about and spoken about. Let me tell a story to explain this.

Ten-year-old Robert was walking his dog one day while drinking a banana milkshake, when suddenly a car crashed into the pavement and ran over his foot. A stranger called an ambulance and Robert was treated for a broken foot.

In the lunch hall at school, many months later, Robert was happily getting his lunch and chatting to friends, when someone accidentally spilt their banana milkshake on him. Robert then yelled as if the car was crushing his foot again, flung his lunch tray onto the floor, curled into a ball and let out blood-curdling screams.

Common triggers are sensory related, for example sounds, sights, feelings and smells, or thoughts such as 'you're going to reject me'. In the story of the boy with the banana milkshake, his trigger was the smell of the milkshake because his subconscious had linked that with the accident, but he probably didn't know that. In a school setting, a child who responds with a brainstem, survival threat response by kicking, screaming, running or hiding would often be expected to immediately discuss the reasons for their behaviour with a teacher. However, the usual cognitive abilities of the child would often not be available due to the overwhelming response of the brainstem. Their thinking, cognitive, intelligent, rational brain response is 'offline', as is their ability to access speech and language.

When adults understand that a child is unable to respond with rational, mature thinking from their prefrontal cortex because their brain is still pumping chemicals that are responding to the threat, then they can employ greater patience and empathy, which in turn helps a child feel safer and recover faster.

When children feel calm and safe, they can focus their energy on learning. Children who are dealing with trauma are often in a chronic state of crisis and fear, and can be in a continual state of threat response; their focus is on trying to feel 'OK' or normal, not on learning information that seems irrelevant to survival. It can be hard for a child to be interested in learning algebra or about a historic war when they are concerned about where their next meal is coming from, if they are going to be in trouble again for forgetting something or who may be gone when they get home.

Trauma impacts a person's behaviour, emotions, relationships and future.

The recovery process

Sometimes it can be hard to work out what recovery actually looks like, so here is a definition of what recovery could be:

> Bad things happened to me, but they no longer have the power to affect how I think and feel or behave. I can now put what happened to me in perspective and move on with my life and when the time comes take my place in society. (Walsh, personal communication, 2016)

Children can recover from trauma but they usually need support to help them process and make sense of the world following their experience.

What you could do

You could speak about the threat response with your child and all learn about the different parts of the brain. You could google 'the triune brain' together, watch films about it and read more about it.

Then, when your child responds with the threat response, you can all speak about it calmly and show empathy rather than being frustrated or worried.

Empathy and emotional connection facilitate healing for a child or young person. Try to connect emotionally with the child in your care when they are expressing strong emotions. The next chapter can help you do that!

Oscar, age seven, was a hard-working student who enjoyed school, friendships and producing good work. Sadly, he was hurt badly by an adult and this affected his school life. He used to run out of the classroom whenever he felt afraid. He started therapy and in this context was able to explore what made him run out, what made him feel afraid and, eventually, what he could do instead of running out of the classroom. He began to feel safe with his therapist and so was able to realise that he ran when he felt ashamed, embarrassed or looked at by other children or adults. He also didn't like big, sudden noises and would often scream and run away. He was eventually able to articulate what scared him and the teacher was able to avoid these things and he stopped running. After about a year of therapy he didn't need to run at all and had been able to explore the abuse that left him with those feelings of fear, shame and nervousness.

Chapter 3

HELPING A CHILD BECOME CALM

If a traumatised child doesn't feel safe and calm then they probably feel scared and tense.

When they feel that, it is likely that they can't recognise those feelings, but will behave in ways that suggest to an adult that they may be feeling anxious.

Until a child feels calm and safe, they can't think and reason very well and can become even more frustrated when adults try and make them speak or act in a logical way.

When they can feel calm, they can begin to reflect and think. They can also begin to repair and heal from the trauma.

An adult can enable a child to recover from trauma by connecting with them emotionally (i.e. being empathetic, kind and attentive and listening to them), which is a great place for them to explore their strong emotions. This can then help them feel less scared about their strong emotions and help them get used to reflecting and articulating their feelings and worries.

For the child to feel safe, emotionally and physically contained (supported) and confident in relating to other people, it is important to empower and help all the adults around the child to facilitate a 'healing environment' by becoming 'therapeutic'.

Every adult can have a positive impact on a traumatised child and help them to recover – whether they are a friend, a lunchtime supervisor, a mentor, an uncle, a teacher or a carer. The skills of empathy, kindness, patience, attunement, listening and valuing each child can change the lives of traumatised children forever and stop the traumatic experience leading to significant problems later on in life.

Can you think of someone who impacted you in your childhood because of their kindness or care?

Bruce Perry is an internationally renowned clinician who helps people understand how to support children who need to recover from experiencing trauma, and he explains that the healing happens both within therapy and the therapeutic environment (school and home). He explains that the brain develops from the bottom up and so the child needs to begin to recover from the bottom of the brain (brainstem) before they can begin to reflect and think about the event (top of the brain – prefrontal cortex). He encourages all of us helping children to focus on being *relational*, *relevant* (relevant to their emotional age), *repetitive*, *rewarding* and *respectful*. This means that when we spend time with traumatised children and focus on the importance of being a supportive adult who is not just 'going through the motions of a role' but really *respects* the child and wants to be a consistent adult in their life, we can help them recover

Butterfly hugs. Cross your arms and pat your back. This is similar to strong sitting and can have the same effect.

A warm drink. Most children will feel better when an attentive, caring adult offers them a warm drink. This can be helpful at any time and can also build a relationship and facilitate a sense of hope and calm.

Favourite smells to smell (in the cosy/safe corner). Smells are really useful ways of bringing fast calm and comfort to a child or young person who feels very frightened, angry, upset or scared. They become associated with safety, and can be hand cream, soap, perfume or aftershave.

Visualisation exercises with pictures that they have drawn (nearby and readily accessible). Draw a happy time, or safe place or have photos of such places.

Spaghetti arms. Tense your body like a stick of dry spaghetti and then relax and be like cooked, wobbly spaghetti. This can help the whole body relax and calm when it has become stiff and painful with anxiety or other strong emotions. Children and young people can also do this when trying to get to sleep at night to relax the body.

Star jumps. This can help a body that is primed to 'fight' be able to release the aggressive energy, feel better and avoid being destructive. Children and young people can be taught to recognise the signs of tension building and then run or do star jumps instead of engaging in a fight or being violent.

The simple art of talking together. Often, traumatised people struggle with words or they come out like a flood but are not really what they think and so can cause hurt. When an adult can listen and not take the words personally but see them as an expression of hurt, then the child or young person can calm down.

Seashell listening or other musical instruments that make similar sounds. Sounds that are associated with safe and lovely times can be calming for a child, just like smells or appropriate touch can.

Swinging outside or in a hammock inside. The movement of swinging can be so helpful, especially when the trauma was experienced when the child or young person was very small. The movement is often comforting, especially when an adult can use a soothing tone of voice to say affirming words such as 'It's OK, it's going to be OK.'

A cosy/safe corner with blankets. This is especially useful if they are anxious, as they get tired more quickly than most children or young people and need to rest and recover. This can help them feel understood and also help them calm down if they are experiencing strong feelings.

Cuddly toys. Have these ready no matter what their age. Cuddly toys can be helpful to bring comfort and calm. They can feel like a comforting hug and no one must be teased for having one when they are an older teen.

Favourite books ready to read together. Familiar books can be a comforting experience for a frightened child whose emotions feel out of control.

Using puppets for the child to express and be a voice for the reason they became dysregulated. Sometimes a child can't express how they feel but a simple animal puppet can ask them and somehow they can find the words. Maybe an animal can tell the child that they have experienced something similar and can talk about how they feel, which can give words to the child to help them explore their feelings. Don't use this method, though, if there is a current court case or a recent disclosure has been made, unless this has been discussed with a professional.

Slime putty or playdough to play with (age relevant). Another sensory experience to help a child feel calm and less overwhelmed. Let the child find out for themselves what sensory toys they like and what they don't like and never make a child play with a sensory object that they feel is unpleasant.

Journalling or scrap books for collaging happy things when a child is overwhelmed by sadness. A happy book can help them remember that there are fun and happy times that they have experienced or will do soon. This can bring a sense of stability, calm and hope to their lives. Some children love to journal by writing or drawing how they feel and then shutting the book. Do respect the child or young person's privacy though, as they can feel violated if you read it without permission, especially after about the age of nine.

Calming music. Listening to the sort of music that can calm a child (chosen beforehand).

Playing a musical instrument (can regulate breathing). When a child feels confident with an instrument they can use it to help them self-regulate and calm themselves down. It can help them feel more in control of their emotions.

Painting can be helpful for a child who finds words tough, and big strokes can help with anger and frustration but can get messy. Smaller strokes can be calming.

A warm bubble bath can bring comfort to a child or young person and help them feel looked after and nurtured.

Playing with a pet can help them feel less isolated and make them feel loved and supported, which can calm them down and help them think and often talk about their feelings.

Going for a walk. Fresh air can help a depressed or anxious child or young person if they feel cared for but not if they feel they are being sent out because the adult can't cope with them. It can help them to feel hopeful again.

Kicking a ball (when angry). Kicking can be a threat response and so sometimes it can be good for a child or young person to kick but in a non-destructive way.

Jumping on a trampoline. Physical exercise of any kind is helpful to calm the person down and release endorphins to help them feel better about life.

Blowing bubbles to each other where you try to catch them. This is a great activity for children to play with an adult to build a relationship and help regulate breathing, which calms them down.

Playing the drums together – using any saucepan or the table! A good way of releasing anger and frustration in a fun way that could lead to laughter, which is healing.

Dancing to some loud music. Another fun exercise to help release all the tension and physical stress.

Marching around the room with them. As above but for younger children.

Distraction: 'Look over there, I wonder if we could…' This can be useful at first when a huge emotional outburst begins, but needs to be followed through with words that soothe and validate the emotions expressed until they can be talked through a little bit.

These activities can be helpful for children or young people who are traumatised and need adults to help them learn how to calm down, relax, think and recover. If you know that the child you are caring for needs to recover from trauma then these are things that you can do with them to help. Try some out and see which ones work with your child. Remember never to force a child or even tell them to do activities in an angry way, as then they'll associate these positive strategies with feelings of fear and powerlessness rather than nurture and care.

Our own strong feelings

It is not easy at all when a child begins to have a meltdown. It can be frightening, threatening and hard to not take personally when a child shouts horrid things at you.

However, it is so vital to remind yourself that traumatised children need to learn that adults can be dependable, caring, patient and loving to counteract the negative messages they have often received in the past.

Those of us who become therapeutic parents or carers for a traumatised child become the child's secure person or, as a researcher called Bowlby suggested years ago, 'a secure base from which to explore the world' (Bowlby, 1988, p.68). We can do this by being emotionally available, sensitive, responsive and helpful. The more we can do that, the faster a child will be able to heal.

To do so means we have to be able to manage our own feelings and stress so that we don't already feel 'emotionally full' and we have some emotional resources available. We need to try to make sure that we are not going to transfer any of our stress and negative emotions to the children.

Therefore, as caretakers, we need to get the support we need to be the best carer that we can be – there's no shame in needing support and time for ourselves.

Often, after a meltdown, it's time for a cup of tea ourselves – or at least a few deep breaths. There needs to be time for the adult to recover and restore too. Maybe you could plan an evening off or a bubble bath with candles for after the children's bedtime?

It is also so important to try and remember that when it looks like things are going wrong, you need to work really hard on not taking it personally. Staying calm enables us to be consistent and supportive, listen to the children, say sorry if necessary, accept and validate their feelings by reflecting them, be 'trigger-aware' and 'body language-aware', avoid labels and telling them what they are feeling, and treasure the moments when things go well.

We usually need the support of other adults who understand this process and can champion us as we invest in the recovery of a traumatised child.

Chapter 4

FRUSTRATING BEHAVIOURS FROM TRAUMATISED CHILDREN

If we can try and understand that the children who are traumatised are essentially 'stuck' internally in a period of time where they didn't have their needs met, it can make their behaviour less strange or disconcerting.

Sadly, until their needs are somehow resolved, they will still look to have them met in the 'here and now'.

It may seem that they are displaying immature behaviour that is inappropriate for their physical appearance or age, but very often their behaviour is just like someone at a very much younger age who is showing strong emotions.

This means that when children or young people of any age demonstrate behaviours that frustrate us, it can help if we realise that they are not trying to irritate or wind us up and we need to work hard to avoid responding to them as if they are!

If we can realise that when they show such frustrating behaviours, it can cause us to feel really shocked and frustrated of course, but this reaction can actually be like pouring petrol on a fire!

Do you know older children who often have tantrums like a two-year-old?

Have you noticed that telling them to 'grow up' and 'act their age' can make their behaviour worse?

Our focus needs to be to make sure we are calm and can appropriately respond as if they are actually the age that they are acting.

For example, we feel relatively used to seeing little ones throwing themselves on the floor with frustration because of silly things happening, like their orange peel not coming off whole – yet such frustrations can actually be the same for ten-year-olds who have been traumatised. They need the same calm, reflective adult response from us, where we are kind, empathetic and help them calm down by our tone of voice and nurturing, firm reactions.

We must avoid shaming them or telling them to grow up or pull themselves together, as that can escalate the behaviour. Once they feel they have been understood and had a nurturing response then you can ask if the child could express those feelings in a different way and help them do so.

Let's look at some other frustrating behaviours you might see.

Attention-seeking

It has been said that if a child needs attention, then maybe we need to give them attention until they don't need it anymore! They will need, depend on and want your company less and less as they become more secure.

Anger

Anger is usually an expression of fear. Rage and emotional outbursts are usually learnt behaviour that has kept them alive in times of extreme fear. It's really hard for traumatised children to regulate their emotions and the only way to help them is to co-regulate – to use calming tones of voice, nurturing but firm words that help them feel safe again and then do calming activities with them. Just like with a two-year-old having a rage fit over something silly, showing patience, empathy and kindness is the key.

Being 'zoned out'

This kind of 'psychological shutdown' response shows us as carers that the child probably gave up having rage outbursts to try and get their needs met and felt utterly powerless, so they had no choice but to 'disappear' into their heads.

Some children just glaze over for a bit and others can shut down different aspects of themselves from emotions and body sensations (sometimes leading to wetting and soiling); others can lose time and have little memory of whole chunks of their life. Ultimately, what they need is safe, kind, nurturing, patient attention until they can explore, with a mental health professional, the reasons for the shutting down. Telling them not to shut down or glaze over will only add shame, so just be patient…

Hyperactive

Sometimes having a therapeutic carer and accessing therapy are still not quite enough to enable some traumatised children to calm sufficiently to fit into school and other such formal environments. Often they are seen as naughty children, but it could be that they were neglected or are just energetic, busy children who will continue like that as adults! Or it could be that when they were little they had to work hard to 'catch' their parent's attention. For many, relaxing would be too frightening an option, as it makes them vulnerable to strong feelings, hypervigilance (being on high alert to every small sound, movement, facial expression, smell or feeling) and the pain of the here and now. Working out some safe activities to help calm them down is essential, alongside working on sleep strategies to help them feel safe at night.

Controlling

Often, carers feel that if a child is controlling then they need to control the environment more strongly in order to stop this. Usually, children who are needing to control things are either living in a strong fear of being powerless in case something terrifying happens again, or they are just used to looking after themselves and taking responsibility that isn't normal for children to take. This means that negotiating control is sensible.

Giving the children options and involving them in decisions is essential to help them feel less scared.

Telling them off or shaming them always escalates the problem. As they relax into the comfort of a carer who is kind, empathetic and helps them reflect, they'll become less controlling.

Chapter 5

KEY APPROACHES TO HELP CHILDREN RECOVER

Empathy

Being empathetic helps to heal a child or young person. Empathy is not sympathy but is the effort of emotionally connecting to them by 'standing in their shoes' and trying to understand how they must be feeling. Studies show that this can radically change the feelings of rejection and low self-worth in a child.

Kindness

It sounds so simple, but when we respond with kindness rather than frustration, irritation, anger, exhaustion or rejection, the child or young person feels safe enough to speak and explore their own responses. Consistent kindness can heal a child who has been through trauma. Being harsh or shouting can be very frightening for children.

Patience

This is sometimes the hardest thing as a parent or carer. It often requires taking deep breaths, thinking through the long-term consequences of not being patient (i.e. more tantrums and louder screams) and being brave and courageous.

Thinking the best/not taking it personally

It's so easy to take it personally when they shout 'I hate you' or 'I won't eat it because it's disgusting'. It takes courage to remember that the words are not spoken in truth but are usually expressions of strong emotions because they feel safe enough to say those things to you.

We often know the theory but it's hard to remind our hearts, isn't it? But when we do, we can be the adult and remain calm, kind and empathetic and respond with calm sentences like, 'You seem to be feeling strong feelings now. I know you don't hate me and I want you to know that I really care for you.'

Being kind to yourself

Somehow, in all of this it is important to do something to look after yourself even if that's going to the gym or making time to meet up with friends.

Taking time to breathe, reflect, think about your responses and think about your needs can really help you to feel less frustrated and hurt and can enable you to have enough emotional energy to cope with the tough behaviour. Exercise can really help your body de-stress and feel strong enough to keep being that relied-on adult.

Having some special time with a child one to one

Find an activity that you and the child enjoy and plan on engaging in this regularly. It could be an activity like fishing, cycling or building dens. It could be enjoying a milkshake or a hot chocolate, nail painting, massage or sharing a special pudding. Whatever it is, it's important that it is fun and something that you both look forward to.

Getting help when you can

It's actually a sign of strength to ask for help when you need it. It's not a weakness at all. It's important to try and make friends with others who are finding parenting or working with traumatised children challenging so that you can share ideas and support each other in the tough times.

Thoughts and tips from other people

Here are some top tips from some of the adults who I have worked with in the Trauma Recovery Centre.

Lucy: Concentrate on the relationship, 'ignore' the behaviour – it's there as a wall to try and stop you getting too close… Self-preservation means they need to keep you at a distance.

Heather: My biggest revelation with my boys at school age was that something like an angry tantrum straight out of school that was being directed at me actually had nothing to do with me and usually meant that something had gone wrong in the day and their crazy behaviour meant they felt safe enough with me to show their real behaviour.

Annie: Remember the importance of empathy for and acknowledgement of the feelings, balanced with boundaries… 'I can see that you are angry and that's a really overwhelming feeling, but it's not OK to hurt others when you're angry.' And the importance of restoring relationships after a bust up – and ways to do that.

Heather: I would say talk to school and keep talking to school about your child, what's happening at home and your child's past. School may not see what you do and if they do (unless they've had fantastic training) they may not understand it. There is so much that schools can do to help children feel safe in school…just help them to know your child better.

Andrew: It's worth investing the time in young lives while they are still young and can recover and change so much quicker than when they are older!

Jennifer: Encourage parents to allow their children to cry and not to say 'don't be sad'. That learned behaviour in a child can take years to unlearn…

Hannah: It's helpful to remember that 'angry' behaviour/words often, but not always, actually mean they're feeling scared, anxious, insecure, embarrassed or ashamed. Anger just feels a much safer, easier thing to express. And also to know that despite anything they may throw at you, what they are in fact desperate for is to be able to trust you, to know you're safe, reliable, consistent and honest.

Sarah: Remember that shame is at their core and as an adult we can help reduce that.

Lucy: It's vital to know calm-down techniques to deal with panic attacks and overwhelming anxiety.

Eila: Keep a sense of humour!

Chapter 6

IMPORTANT THINGS TO CONSIDER WHEN TRYING TO FACILITATE RECOVERY

Resilience

Resilience is a word that is really important to mention when exploring the impact that trauma can have on a child.

Have you noticed that when children or adults experience the same dreadful events some seem to 'bounce back' quickly and others seem to be really significantly knocked by the experience?

There are several factors involved in building a child's resilience. The most important factor is the attachment that they have with their primary caregiver or key adult(s).

When they can trust that their needs will be met, that they are loved and that they are listened to and cared for, they have a greater capacity to 'bounce back' from difficult situations or events.

Attachment

This word 'attachment' is now beginning to be a common word that people use when discussing how young children relate to their primary caregiver – usually their mum or dad (but not always).

It is a word that describes the bond between them and how that bond makes the young children feel about the world. It is now understood really clearly from research studies that when a primary caregiver is able to ensure that the babies and young children (especially in the first five years) have their needs met by an adult or adults who are emotionally engaged and emotionally present, playful and nurturing, then the child is less likely to be as deeply impacted by some emotional challenges later on in life.

The other ways to help a child build resilience are summarised in the acronym: RESPIRE.

Relationships: are key to strength.

Empathy: children need empathy to then be able to be empathetic.

Strengths and weaknesses: knowing what they are good at and what they struggle with.

Processing life together: the ups and downs are explored with another adult.

Inner confidence: feeling happy with themselves and who they are.

Responsibility: able to make good choices.

Empowerment to make a difference: able to make a difference to society.

(de Thierry, 2015)

Maybe there are other siblings who are not struggling emotionally or are not showing behaviour challenges at the moment, but this understanding can help to build up their resilience when it is applied to daily life.

Saying sorry

When we are involved in any relationship, saying sorry is central to things working well. It's the oil of relationships.

When we are caring for traumatised children, saying sorry is a really important thing to do. We can't always be the patient, kind, nurturing, attentive, attuned adult that these children need, but we can say sorry when we respond wrongly, are less than patient or lose energy.

When we say sorry and explain that what we did or said wasn't great and how we feel sad about it, we are enabling repair to happen.

Not only does this then repair the relationship, it also models healthy rupture-repair relationship experiences to the children that they can follow for the rest of their lives.

Their behaviour

Children who have been traumatised often behave in ways that can shock and upset people.

They can lie, they can hurt others and they can deny ever hurting others or doing things that you even saw that they did.

They can make up stories about what they did or what you did that can really hurt and frustrate. They can seem to be purposefully trying to annoy the adult but because we know that all behaviour is communication, we know that we need to try and not take it personally and instead work out what's going on.

Children often lie because their reality can be too difficult to explain or think about. It's easier to pretend that you are a millionaire if your family is struggling with money. People seem to be more empathetic when a child says that they experienced a road accident or have a parent who is sick and yet there can be little support available when a child says that they are frightened of their parents or they are mentally ill. So children lie.

Memory is affected when someone is traumatised too. Sometimes a child may be lying when they say they didn't do something, but sometimes they really can't remember. When any of us go into shock, our memories don't store the events very well and words are often really hard to find.

Chapter 7

GETTING YOUR HEAD AROUND THE DIFFERENT THERAPIES ON OFFER

The recovery process will often need the intervention of therapy and there are different approaches that have evidence of facilitating recovery.

It is important to understand that any intervention for trauma needs to start off as primarily non-verbal for children, to enable the trauma that is 'held' in the subconscious to be explored. As I explained earlier in the book, the speech and language part of the brain called the Broca's area, goes 'offline' during a traumatic experience, along with the rational part of the brain, the prefrontal cortex, and so they are not that helpful for processing trauma. Creative therapies, which don't depend on verbal processing, can help significantly. It is also important to recognise that often the parents or carers need support and help to understand the impact of trauma too.

Individual therapies are the backbone of trauma recovery, as they offer individually tailored programmes of therapy to promote recovery and resilience.

Creative therapies are essential for enabling the non-verbal memories or the traumatic experiences which have caused the Broca's area of the brain, which is responsible for speech and language, to shut down. When someone is rendered 'speechless' due to the intensity of the trauma and the powerful nature of the brainstem response of fight, fright or freeze, creative therapy can give language to the experience and begin to make sense of it (psychotherapy, art therapy, music therapy, play therapy).

Verbal therapies can be helpful for processing trauma and enabling a cognitive response to be developed as part of the child's transforming narrative once the child has become calm, stabilised and safe. Young people often need time to talk through their feelings and experience.

Group therapies can be helpful to bring together children with similar experiences and give them the opportunity to receive support and learn from each other. This can reduce the isolation that trauma can cause.

Family therapies can be helpful for children who are returning to their family of origin to help them create a safe and healing family unit to facilitate recovery. Or they can help to build positive attachments in the family unit after a traumatic period of time.

Therapeutic communities are an intervention that can facilitate recovery by providing a 'holding' environment that can enable a child to grow and recover from some of the harm done to them.

It is recognised that *short-term interventions* can be appropriate for children who have experienced one-off incidents of trauma, but for children who have experienced longer-term or interpersonal trauma, longer-term therapeutic intervention is essential and short-term intervention can be counter productive. A child or young person may begin to feel relieved that they can trust an adult in the therapy setting, but then after the therapy is over they are unable to see them again and this can lead to further trauma and loss.

Therapy significantly differs from therapeutic work because in therapy a client will work with the therapist to try to understand the unconscious responses and will process and gain insight into their situation and understanding about themselves. Over time this processing and integrating of experiences and feelings enables the symptoms of the trauma to reduce. The overall aim is to enable a client to change and grow on a personal level in a safe and facilitating environment. The relationship between the therapist and the client is of central importance.

Therapeutic work and mentoring aim to work only with what is already known and not with the unconscious. They aim to enable practical skill development and build self-esteem and self-confidence. Working in a mentoring group can also enable clients to negotiate social isolation and build social skills.

Therapy and mentoring activities are on different ends of a spectrum but both can be helpful for the child to have a full recovery. The therapeutic interventions form an essential foundational base for a child, while therapy is essential to explore the unconscious responses that can be confusing.

Conclusion

It is possible for children and young people to recover from trauma. It's so helpful when the adults can recognise the behaviour and emotional responses that present as trauma symptoms, as this can immediately reduce shame and empower the survivor to understand themselves more and feel less anxious.

We can bring transformation to many families and communities when we work hard at supporting those who have been traumatised, as they will then grow up to be emotionally intelligent, confident, self-aware young adults who will be equipped with so much to help them lead fulfilling lives in adulthood.

Well done to you all. We can do this!

REFERENCES

Bowlby, J. (1988) *A Secure Base: Clinical Applications of Attachment Theory.* London: Routledge.

Institute of Recovery from Childhood Trauma (IRCT) (2015) Our Theoretical Underpinnings. Available at www.irct.org.uk, accessed on 25 July 2016.

Levine, P. and Kline, M. (2007) *Trauma through a Child's Eyes: Awakening the Ordinary Miracle of Healing.* Berkeley, CA: North Atlantic Books.

Oaklander, V. (2001) 'Gestalt play therapy.' *International Journal of Play Therapy 10, 2,* 44–55.

Perry, B. and Szalavitz, M. (2011) *Born for Love: Why Empathy Is Essential – and Endangered.* New York: HarperCollins.

de Thierry, B. (2015) *Teaching the Child on the Trauma Continuum.* Guildford: Grosvenor Publishing.

Walsh, M. (2016) Definition of recovery given in a discussion with Institute of Recovery from Childhood Trauma (IRCT) trustees.

RECOMMENDED FURTHER READING

Cozolino, L. (2006) *The Neuroscience of Human Relationships: Attachment and the Social Brain*. New York: Norton Publishers.

Perry, B. and Szalavitz, M. (2011) *Born for Love: Why Empathy Is Essential – and Endangered*. New York: HarperCollins.

Seigel, D. and Payne Bryson, T. (2012) *The Whole-Brain Child: Twelve Proven Strategies to Nurture Your Child's Developing Mind*. New York: Delacorte Press.

de Thierry, B. (2015) *Teaching the Child on the Trauma Continuum*. Guildford: Grosvenor Publishing.

HELPFUL ORGANISATIONS AND RESOURCES TO SUPPORT YOU AS YOU SUPPORT A TRAUMATISED CHILD OR YOUNG PERSON

Betsy de Thierry is a director of these organisations:

Betsy de Thierry Ltd is the trauma training, leadership and consultancy company that has started many charities to help traumatised children. BdT Ltd offers training to schools, residential homes, foster parents, police, therapy centres and any other organisation that works with traumatised children and young people. It also offers consultancy to those working with trauma.

www.betsytraininguk.co.uk

Institute of Recovery from Childhood Trauma (IRCT) is an umbrella organisation that exists to ensure that recovery from childhood trauma is available for all.

www.irct.org.uk

Trauma Recovery Centre (TRC) offers therapy for traumatised children and young people and alternative education for traumatised children. It also offers training.

www.trc-uk.org

UK national resources for traumatised children

NSPCC is a UK charity that offers resources to support families across the nation. It has training courses, programmes for families to get support and good resources to download.

www.nspcc.org.uk

NWG Network is aimed at supporting professionals working with traumatised children and young people, especially those who have experienced child sexual exploitation or trafficking.

www.nwgnetwork.org

Young Minds has great resources to help you support children and young people who are struggling with mental health challenges. It describes itself as 'the voice for young people's health and wellbeing'.

www.youngminds.org.uk

Expert help from around the world

Child Trauma Academy offers expertise on trauma and its impact on children through courses, books and newsletters.

www.childtrauma.org

The European Society for Trauma and Dissociation (ESTD) and the **International Society for the Study of Trauma and Dissociation (ISSTD)** offer expertise on complex trauma and have a fact sheet for teachers to download.

www.estd.org and www.isst-d.org

The National Child Traumatic Stress Network also has great resources for teachers and parents about trauma and supporting the traumatised child.

www.nctsn.org

The Post Institute helps traumatised children and young people. It is a 'love-based family-centred approach to helping children with challenging behaviours'.

www.postinstitute.com

Looking for a therapist?

Looking for a therapist for a child? Here are some UK national organisations that can help with this.

To find therapists in other nations please contact the organisations listed in 'Expert help from around the world' along with a few listed below.

British Association for Music Therapy
www.bamt.org

British Association of Counsellors and Psychotherapists
www.bacpregister.org.uk

British Association of Play Therapists
www.bapt.info/find-therapist

Gestalt London
http://gpti.org.uk

Register of Play and Creative Arts Therapists
www.playtherapyregister.org.uk

The British Association of Art Therapists
www.baat.org

UK Council for Psychotherapy
http://members.psychotherapy.org.uk/findATherapist

Therapists from other nations
Play Therapy International (PTI)
www.playtherapy.org

INDEX

from trauma. The consistency is vital for the child, alongside shared, *repetitive, relationally rewarding* experiences like playing, walking the dog, cooking or some other experience that is frequent and enjoyable for both adult and child. Traumatised children often get emotionally 'stuck' when they get terrified and the age at which they are 'stuck' at is often the age they still act when they are scared, no matter how long it's been since the original trauma. So a 13-year-old who was abused when he was five years old may still act like a five-year-old when he is scared or angry, and this is called his emotional age. The shared, fun experience needs to be relevant to the emotional age of the child rather than their biological age.

Someone who is a consistent, caring adult, shows that they care and takes time to communicate in a way that is predictable, clear, respectful and kind can change the child's life. It's relationships like these that reshape the brain of the traumatised child.

Violet Oaklander is a child therapist who was one of the original pioneers of therapy for children. She spoke of how central these relationships are in the recovery from trauma. When speaking about recovering from trauma, she says: 'Nothing happens without at least a thread of a relationship. The relationship is a tenuous thing that takes careful nurturing. It is the foundation of the therapeutic process and can, in and of itself, be powerfully therapeutic' (Oaklander, 2001, p.46).

How to help a child self-regulate

Sometimes a child can become upset, have a tantrum or look as if they have 'lost the plot'.

It can take the smallest thing for them to become emotionally overwhelmed and the atmosphere can change to really tense and quickly escalate to a huge 'scene'.

Usually it happens because the child wanted their own way. This is normal, developmentally appropriate behaviour in preschool children, but if the children have experienced trauma in the past, they may be re-experiencing strong negative feelings of powerlessness or fear, be unsure how to express themselves and so use regressive behaviour.

There are so many reasons why a child may escalate emotionally and it's useful to learn, as caretakers, how to help a child calm down and be able to stop an emotional outburst becoming a huge, painful situation.

So, here are some ideas for soothing and calming a child when they are having an emotional outburst or they are zoned out, shut down or experiencing strong negative emotions. They need to be held as ideas for children according to the emotional age of the child at that time, and for those of us working with traumatised children, these are the foundational soothing activities for times of stress and difficulty.

I recommend these ideas to the families that I work with; they use the five senses to help children who are feeling stressed, upset or emotionally dysregulated.

I have seen these ideas introduce some real safety to the homes of families recovering from trauma. When they are done with a warm, empathetic, kind, attuned, nurturing adult who doesn't shout at them or make them feel bad about their behaviour, the activities and strategies also help a child to recover from trauma.

Why don't you take a look through the ideas below and try some of them?

Breathing exercises. This is vital to help all children calm down from stress, crisis or trauma. We should all practise spending time breathing calmly and speaking kindly to ourselves. Breathe deeply in through your nose and out through your mouth for a longer breath.

Square breathing. Imagine a square and breathe in slowly through your nose for a count of four. Hold your breath for a count of four and then breathe out through your mouth for a count of four. Hold for a count of four. (It's important that you breathe out for longer than you breathe in.)

A sensory toy to squeeze, cuddle or go to. This can calm a child down when they feel really angry, sad or upset. It can be a 'transitionary object' that someone who they love or feel safe with gave them or it can just be something that they chose that they like. Children eventually do this naturally to comfort or calm themselves. Some children have a small object in their pocket all day long to reassure them.

Strong sitting exercises. Put your two arms outstretched in front of you. Cross them over and hold your hands together. Bring your hands under towards your chest and squeeze together while doing breathing exercises. This feels like a big hug and can be very calming and comforting for a child or youth. It also stimulates both parts of the brain, which aids recovery, so we call it brain gym; the science name is 'bilateral stimulation'.